Digging Up the Dead

OSSUARIES and CHARNEL HOUSES

By Greg Roza

Gareth Stevens
PUBLISHING

Please visit our website, www.garethstevens.com. For a free color catalog of all our high-quality books, call toll free 1-800-542-2595 or fax 1-877-542-2596.

Library of Congress Cataloging-in-Publication Data

Roza, Greg.
Ossuaries and charnel houses / by Greg Roza.
p. cm. — (Digging up the dead)
Includes index.
ISBN 978-1-4824-1270-3 (pbk.)
ISBN 978-1-4824-1233-8 (6-pack)
ISBN 978-1-4824-1487-5 (library binding)
1. Ossuaries — History. 2. Tombs — Juvenile literature. 3. Death — Social aspects — Juvenile literature. I. Roza, Greg. II. Title.
GT3320.R69 2015
363.7—d23

First Edition

Published in 2015 by
Gareth Stevens Publishing
111 East 14th Street, Suite 349
New York, NY 10003

Designer: Andrea Davison-Bartolotta
Editor: Greg Roza

Photo credits: Cover, p. 1 DEA/M. Borchi/De Agostini/Getty Images; cover, back cover, pp. 1–32 (background dirt texture) Kues/Shutterstock.com; pp. 4, 6, 8, 10, 13, 14, 16, 18, 21, 23, 25, 27, 29 (gravestone) jayfish/Shutterstock.com; p. 4 DEA/ A. Dagli Orti/De Agostini/Getty Images; p. 5 © iStockphoto.com/Studio-Annika; p. 6 Robert F. Sisson/National Geographic/Getty Images; p. 7 Maxim Tarasyugin/ Shutterstock.com; p. 9 (both) Matjaz Krivic/Getty Images; p. 11 British Library/ Robana via Getty Images; pp. 12–13 Wyatt Rivard/Shutterstock.com; p. 13 (inset) Deror avi/Wikimedia Commons; p. 14 Jim Dyson/Getty Images; p. 15 Ashok Sinha/ Photolibrary/Getty Images; pp. 16, 17 (top, bottom) Giorgio Cosulich/Getty Images; p. 17 (middle) Richard Ross/Stockbyte/Getty Images; p. 18 (left) Mikhail Markovskiy/ Shutterstock.com; pp. 18 (right), 19 Marcel Gross/Shutterstock.com; p. 21 Michal Cizek/AFP/Getty Images; p. 22 Nuno Sequeira André/Wikimedia Commons; p. 23 © iStockphoto.com/Silvrshootr; p. 24 Ulrich Baumgarten via Getty Images; p. 25 Jean-Christophe Verhaegen/AFP/Getty Images; p. 26 Robert Harding World Imagery/Getty Images; p. 27 tenten10/Shutterstock.com; pp. 28–29 Paradiso/ Wikimedia Commons.

Printed in the United States of America

CPSIA compliance information: Batch #CS15GS: For further information contact Gareth Stevens, New York, New York at 1-800-542-2595.

CONTENTS

Words in the glossary appear in **bold** type the first time they are used in the text.

HOUSE OF BONES

Originally, an ossuary (AH-shuh-wehr-ee) was a jar or box used to hold bones, usually those of a single person. In time, the word became used for chambers, rooms, and even whole buildings where human bones were kept. Today, the term "ossuary" is more often used for locations where the bones of dead people are honored or displayed for the public to see.

Iron Age ossuary

Charnel houses are very similar to ossuaries, but perhaps less fancy. A charnel house is simply a place where bones are deposited. The bones in many charnel houses were eventually used to make ossuaries for honoring the dead. Some of these are monuments today. Ossuaries are usually more artistically designed, with the bones sometimes used for actual decoration.

GRAVE MATTERS

The word "charnel" comes from the Latin word *carnis*, which means "of the flesh." "Ossuary" comes from the Latin word for bones—*ossua*.

We're Running Out of Room!

One of the most common reasons for charnel houses and ossuaries is a lack of burial space. In some cultures where burial space was limited, people were buried for several years—long enough for the flesh to rot away. Then, the bones were **exhumed** and deposited into a charnel house. This made more room in the ground for newly dead bodies. Some cultures stored the remains of a single person in small boxes, while others piled countless bones in a communal area.

Ossuaries are sometimes called bone houses. Charnel houses are sometimes called **mortuary** chapels.

Ancient ossuaries and charnel houses have been discovered in many locations around the globe, from Europe and Asia to the Americas. Some cultures still use them, and you might be wondering why. There are several **ghastly** yet interesting reasons.

The robed bones of a 6th-century monk have kept watch over the ossuary at Saint Catherine's Monastery for a long, long time.

GRAVE MATTERS

In the 1818 novel *Frankenstein*, Dr. Frankenstein, the scientist who creates the monster, tells readers where he found body parts: "I collected bones from charnel-houses; and disturbed, with **profane** fingers, the tremendous secrets of the human frame."

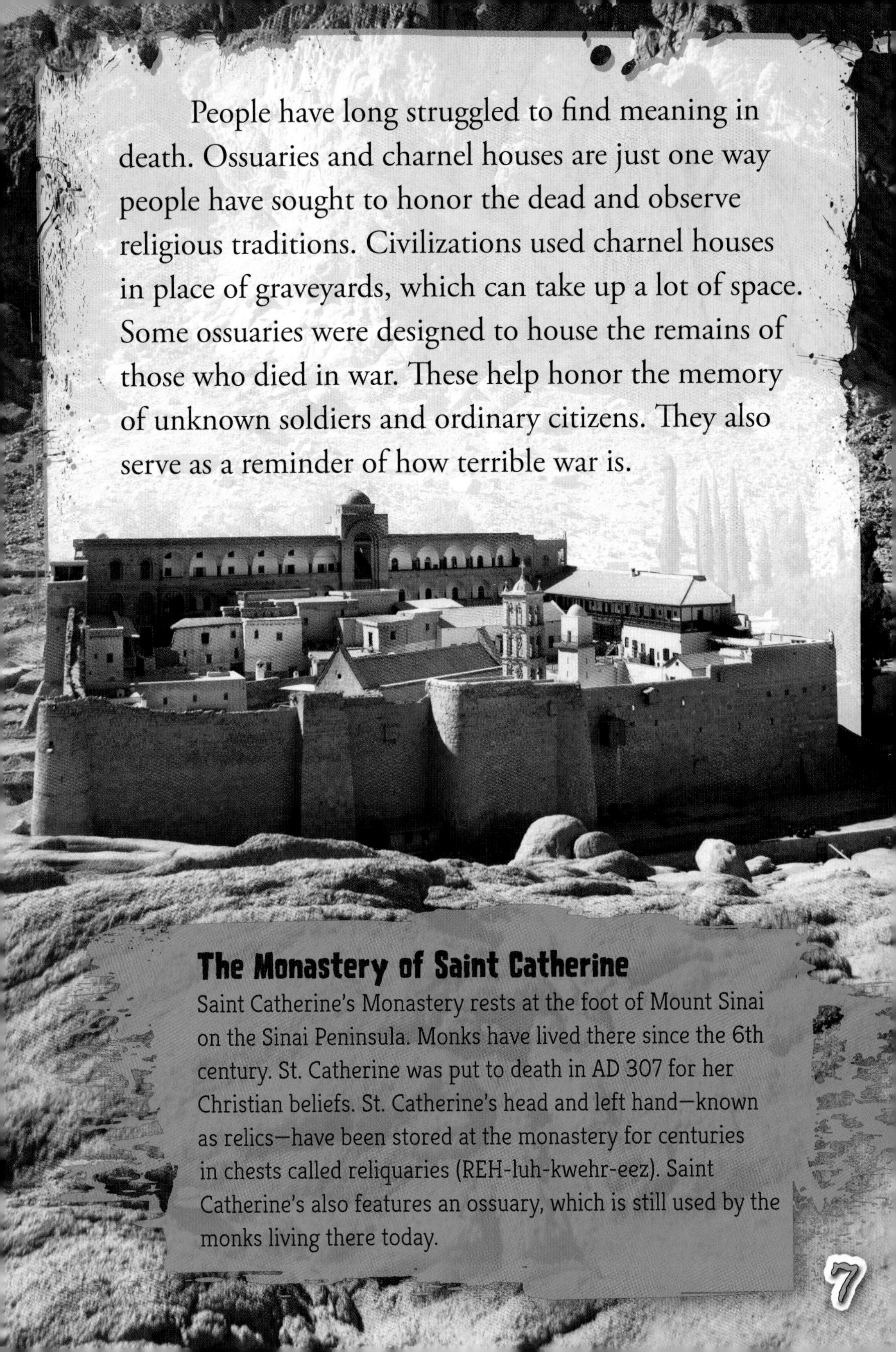

People have long struggled to find meaning in death. Ossuaries and charnel houses are just one way people have sought to honor the dead and observe religious traditions. Civilizations used charnel houses in place of graveyards, which can take up a lot of space. Some ossuaries were designed to house the remains of those who died in war. These help honor the memory of unknown soldiers and ordinary citizens. They also serve as a reminder of how terrible war is.

The Monastery of Saint Catherine

Saint Catherine's Monastery rests at the foot of Mount Sinai on the Sinai Peninsula. Monks have lived there since the 6th century. St. Catherine was put to death in AD 307 for her Christian beliefs. St. Catherine's head and left hand—known as relics—have been stored at the monastery for centuries in chests called reliquaries (REH-luh-kwehr-eez). Saint Catherine's also features an ossuary, which is still used by the monks living there today.

TOWER OF SILENCE

Some of the oldest ossuaries are located in the deserts of Iran and the surrounding area. Zoroastrianism (zawr-uh-WAHS-tree-uh-nih-zuhm) is a religion founded in Persia (ancient Iran) about 3,500 years ago. Zoroastrians honor a god named Ahura Mazda. They believe he is the source of all that's good, including the beauty of the natural world.

When Zoroastrians die, they believe the body becomes a source of evil. Zoroastrians prevent dead bodies from coming into contact with soil, water, and fire. Instead, the bodies are placed on a stone structure called a *dakhma*, or tower of silence. Birds pick the bodies clean, and the sun bleaches the bones. Then, all bones are deposited in an ossuary, which is usually a well in the center of the *dakhma*. Sometimes the bones are ground up first.

GRAVE MATTERS

Tens of thousands of people around the world still practice Zoroastrianism, and some still use ossuaries. Some now cremate, or burn, their dead instead, which is against the traditional beliefs of the religion.

The *Dakhmas* of Mumbai

During the 10th century, many Zoroastrians moved from Persia to India. About 70,000 still live there today. Mumbai, India, is home to three functioning *dakhmas*. However, there's a problem. The local vulture population was badly hurt by man-made chemicals. There aren't enough vultures left to eat the flesh of the dead that are laid out there. Indian Zoroastrians plan to build two aviaries, which are large homes for many birds, in the hopes of bringing vultures back to Mumbai.

This tower of silence in Yazd, Iran, was used as an ossuary up until the 20th century. Now, Zoroastrians in the area bury their dead in concrete coffins.

NATIVE AMERICAN CHARNEL HOUSES

Some Native American groups used charnel houses, particularly eastern tribes of North America. Often, these chambers contained multiple **decomposing** bodies. In time, the bones of these bodies may have been buried in a mass grave. In other cases, Indian groups built great earthen mounds, and sometimes they buried the bones of important people in them. More and more Native American ossuaries are surfacing as erosion and new construction projects uncover them.

In many Choctaw communities, recently dead bodies were placed on a raised platform. Once the flesh was rotten, special people called "bone pickers" removed it from the bones. The bones were washed and stored in a container. Periodically, tribes would place the bones of their loved ones in a communal grave.

GRAVE MATTERS

In 1979, Edward Kaeser revealed that he had uncovered a significant Native American charnel house in a popular city park in the Bronx, New York. The ossuary contained 21 skulls and numerous bones, including dog bones.

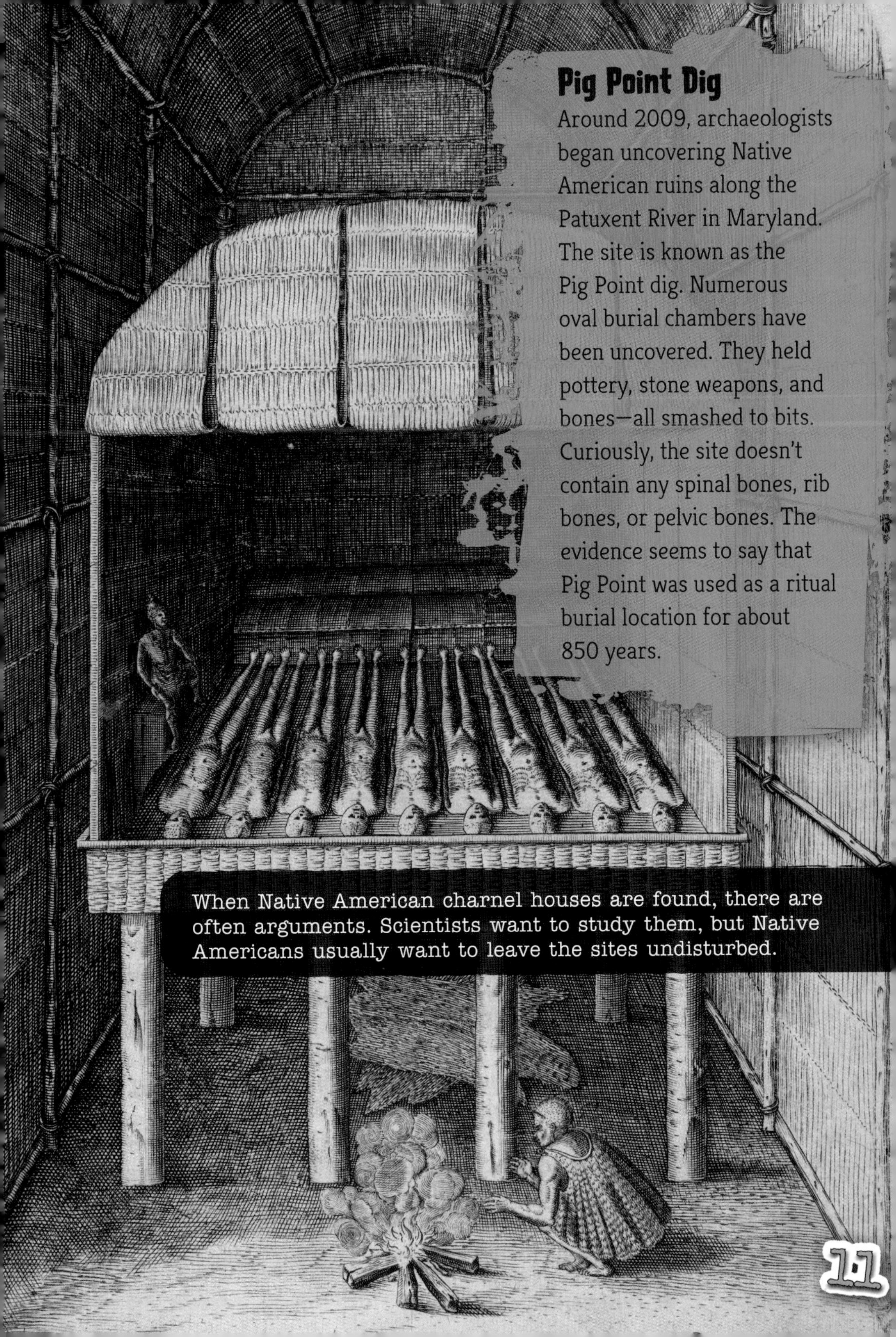

Pig Point Dig

Around 2009, archaeologists began uncovering Native American ruins along the Patuxent River in Maryland. The site is known as the Pig Point dig. Numerous oval burial chambers have been uncovered. They held pottery, stone weapons, and bones—all smashed to bits. Curiously, the site doesn't contain any spinal bones, rib bones, or pelvic bones. The evidence seems to say that Pig Point was used as a ritual burial location for about 850 years.

When Native American charnel houses are found, there are often arguments. Scientists want to study them, but Native Americans usually want to leave the sites undisturbed.

CREEPY CATACOMBS

Beneath the city streets of Paris is a maze of tunnels—or **catacombs**—created when workers mined limestone to build the city. During the late 1700s, the many graveyards in Paris had become so overcrowded that bodies were literally breaking into people's basements! In 1778, the Holy Innocents Cemetery, the largest graveyard in the city, became the first to begin moving remains into the catacombs, officially turning them into a charnel house.

The Paris catacombs are an example of a charnel house created solely for the public health. Today, it's the largest ossuary in the world. The dark corridors hold the remains of 6 million people, perhaps more. Tall, orderly stacks of skulls and bones line the walls of the catacombs, creating a ghastly mood.

Parts of the catacombs are open for tourists. However, people have long snuck into closed sections without permission.

Ossuary Celebrities

Many, many unknown people are buried in the Paris catacombs, but you can find a few historic figures down there as well, particularly French artists. People who fought in the French Revolution (1789–1799) were buried in the catacombs right away. Out of all the remains, there's just one tombstone in the catacombs. It belongs to Françoise Géllain, a woman who spent much of her life trying to get a man released from jail.

GRAVE MATTERS

A sign above one entrance to the Paris ossuary warns visitors, *Arrête! C'est ici l'empire de la mort*. This means, "Halt! This is the realm of Death."

The Iglesia de San Francisco (Church of Saint Francis) in the city of Lima, Peru, was completed in 1774. It's known for its extensive collection of religious books, some of which date back to the 1600s. However, the church is best known for the catacombs, and bones, beneath it.

The catacombs were Lima's first graveyard. They were used for this purpose until 1808, when a graveyard was built outside the city. The catacombs were forgotten until 1947, when they were rediscovered. The hallways of the catacombs are mazelike, cramped, and lined with the bones of Lima's earliest residents. Visitors will also find deep pits dug into the earth, filled with skulls and femur bones arranged in artistic patterns.

GRAVE MATTERS

The bones of an estimated 70,000 to 75,000 people rest in the catacombs of Iglesia de San Francisco.

The bright yellow Iglesia de San Francisco was built in the richly decorated Spanish baroque style. The church and its catacombs are among the most popular tourist attractions in Lima.

Making Room

In 1655, an earthquake caused the original church to fall over. Even before this, religious figures were buried in the catacombs beneath Lima. By the time Iglesia de San Francisco was constructed, the bones of common people were also being placed in the catacombs. The maze of halls filled up with dead bodies. To make more room, newly deceased bodies were covered with **quicklime**, which quickly reduced them to skeletons.

In 1631, the Capuchin (KAA-pyuh-shun) monks of Rome were given land to build a new **friary**. The monks dug up the bones of 4,000 monks and took them to the new location. The bones were placed in the catacombs beneath the newly constructed friary. Around 1700, the monks began to arrange the bones in artistic patterns and shapes. Today, this ossuary is known as the Capuchin Crypt.

The Capuchin catacombs are made up of six rooms connected by a long hallway. One room is a chapel. The rest hold thousands of bones. The rooms have grim names, such as the Crypt of the Pelvises and the Crypt of the Skulls. In each room, the walls and ceilings are covered with shapes, fixtures, and figures made from the monks' bones.

GRAVE MATTERS

American writer Nathaniel Hawthorne visited the Capuchin Crypt, and it had a deep effect on him. He wrote, "Not here can we feel ourselves immortal."

Crypt of the Three Skeletons

The last room, the Crypt of the Three Skeletons, has the most intricate bone decorations. On the ceiling is an oval of **vertebrae** surrounding a skeleton holding a scythe, a symbol of death, and scales, a symbol of God's judgment. The other two skeletons mentioned in the room's name are two children sitting on an altar made of pelvis bones. One holds a spear and the other holds an hourglass, which is a reminder of the shortness of life. There are also several robed skeletons in the room.

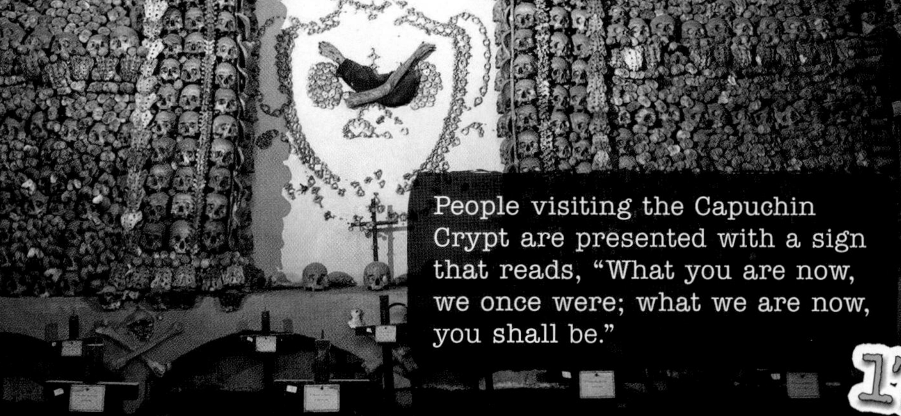

People visiting the Capuchin Crypt are presented with a sign that reads, "What you are now, we once were; what we are now, you shall be."

CZECH OSSUARIES

There are many ossuaries in Europe, and several amazing examples are found in the Czech Republic. The Sedlec Ossuary in Kutná Hora, Czech Republic, might be the most artistic ossuary ever made. It holds the bones of about 40,000 people. It's popularly known as the Bone Church.

In 1870, the wealthy Schwarzenberg family hired a local woodcarver named František Rint to arrange the bones. He bleached the bones so they were all the same color. Then he painstakingly arranged them in artistic patterns and shapes. Rint made a Schwarzenberg coat of arms, ornate candleholders, and giant vases. Perhaps most famous is the bone chandelier Rint made, which contains at least one of every bone in the human body.

GRAVE MATTERS

Rint was a true artist. He even signed his work... in finger bones, of course!

bone chandelier

Dying to Get In

In the 13th century, an abbot from the Sedlec Ossuary visited Jerusalem and brought back a handful of dirt from the Holy Land. He spread the dirt around the Sedlec cemetery. After that, it became a very popular burial place. In the 17th century, after about 30,000 people had been buried there, the older graves were dug up to make room for the newly dead. The older bones were used to make the ossuary.

The Schwarzenberg coat of arms features a raven, made of bones, eating the eye from the skull of an enemy soldier.

The Ossuary of St. James in Brno, Czech Republic, is one of the largest ossuaries in the world, holding the bones of about 50,000 people. In 2001, archaeologists working under the streets of Brno discovered the extensive ossuary beneath the 13th-century church.

Officials knew the area was once used as a graveyard. However, as the graves became too crowded, bones were unearthed so new bodies could be buried. The bones were placed neatly in underground rooms and hallways that could be reached through the church. This practice continued until the 18th century, when the ossuary was so full of bones that no more could be placed in it, and the entrance was sealed. Once the ossuary was opened in 2001, archaeologists were shocked to see how many bones it actually holds.

Painted Skulls

Some ossuaries in western Europe feature skulls painted with family names or images. In the small town of Křtiny, Czech Republic, the Church of the Blessed Virgin Mary has a special basement that holds the bones of about 1,000 people. This ossuary was discovered in the 1990s and restored. It's the only ossuary discovered so far in the Czech Republic with painted skulls. Some are decorated with black laurel leaves and the letter T. No one really knows why yet.

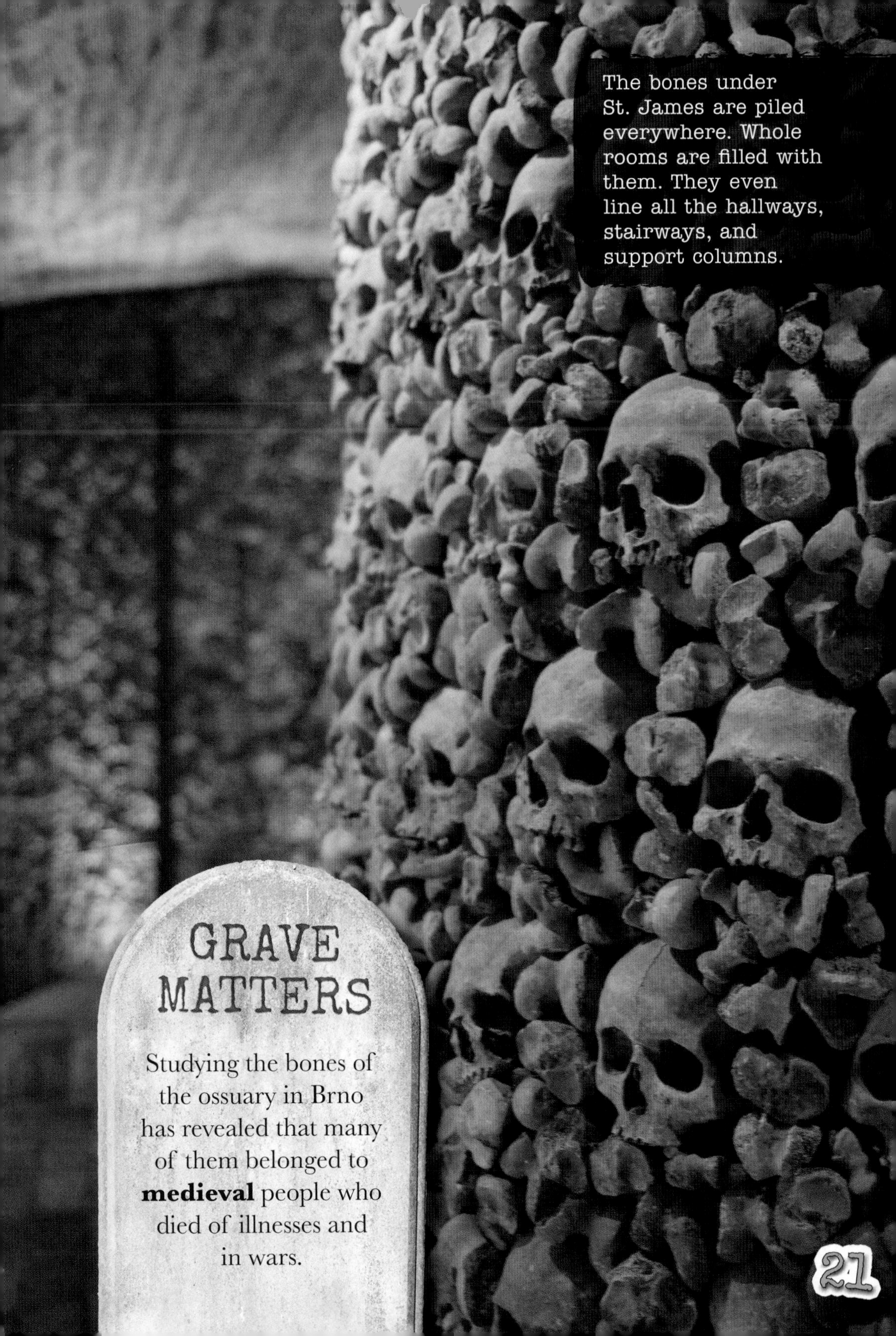

The bones under St. James are piled everywhere. Whole rooms are filled with them. They even line all the hallways, stairways, and support columns.

GRAVE MATTERS

Studying the bones of the ossuary in Brno has revealed that many of them belonged to **medieval** people who died of illnesses and in wars.

CHAPEL OF BONES

The Capela dos Ossos, or Chapel of Bones, can be found at the Church of St. Francis in Evora, Portugal. In the 16th century, the town of Evora had more than 40 cemeteries, which took up a lot of land. When officials decided to destroy several cemeteries, Franciscan monks exhumed the remains of about 5,000 monks. The remains were relocated to the Church of St. Francis. The monks decided to display the bones as a warning to the people of Evora that their lives wouldn't last forever.

The bones were organized in uniform patterns along the walls of the chapel. No matter where you look, the skulls of the long dead stare back at you. The monks hoped to convince people to lead a good life before they died.

A Chilling Reminder

The entrance to the Chapel of Bones bears the Portuguese words: *Nós ossos que aqui estamos, pelos vossos esperamos.* This means, "Our bones that are here wait for yours." This was meant to remind churchgoers that life is short. Visitors will find other religious phrases in Latin among the bones and skulls, such as: "I leave, but I don't die," "I die in the light," and "The day that I die is better than the day that I was born."

Monks used concrete to fasten the skulls and bones to the walls of the chapel.

GRAVE MATTERS

The Chapel of Bones also contains two skeletons hanging by chains. One is a woman, and one is a child. No one is sure why they're there.

BONES OF THE WAR DEAD

The Battle of Verdun was the longest and bloodiest battle of World War I (1914–1918). Between February and December 1916, French and German forces fought on about 7.7 square miles (20 sq km) of hilly countryside near Verdun, France. New weapons such as poison gas and flamethrowers contributed to the death count as the two armies battled back and forth. Some experts believe more than 300,000 soldiers died there.

Today, the Douaumont Ossuary stands where the Battle of Verdun was fought. It was named after the nearby fort German forces occupied in 1916. Inside are the bones of 130,000 unidentified French and German soldiers who died during the battle. Douaumont is also a national cemetery where French soldiers are **interred** in graves and tombs.

Douaumont Ossuary

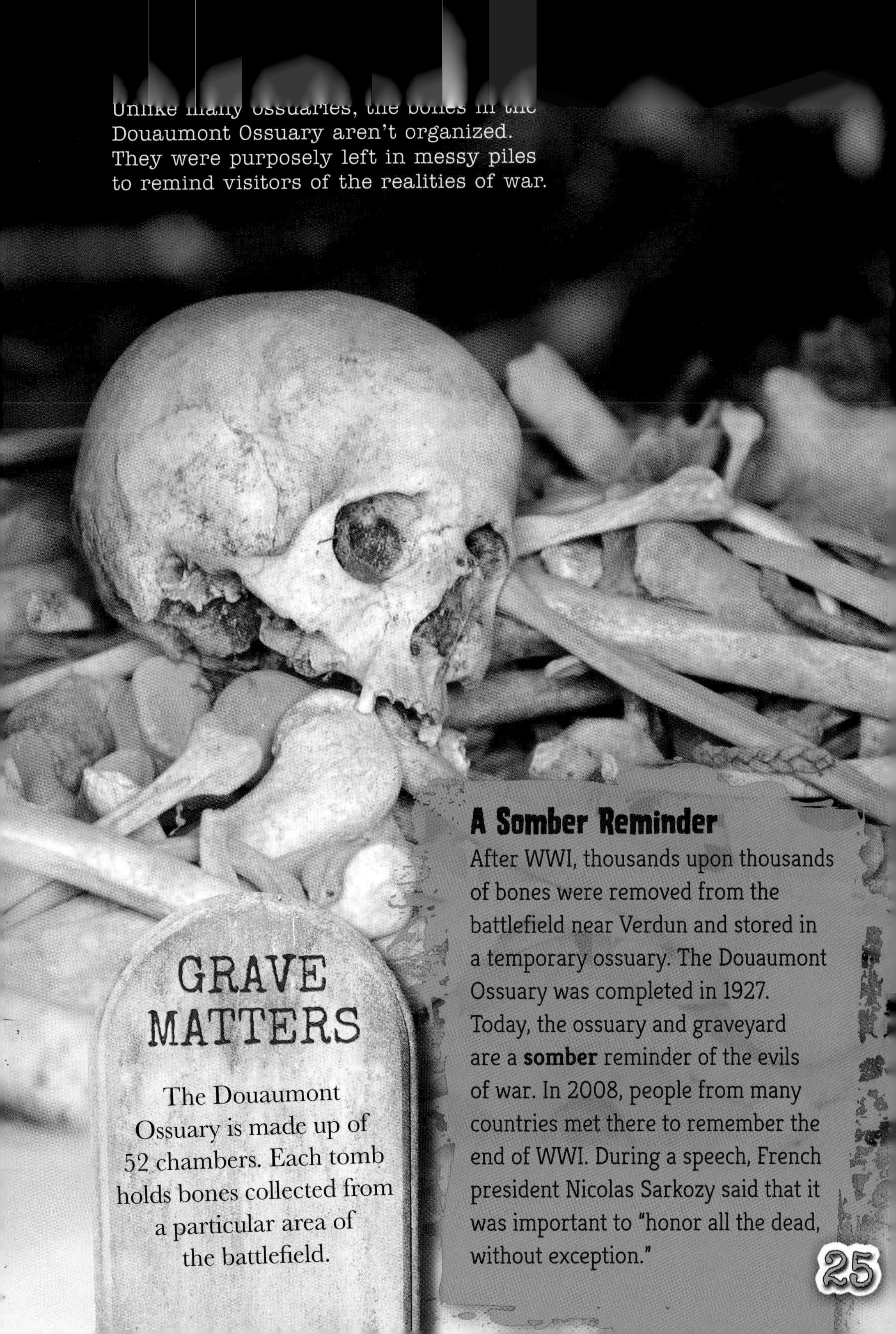

Unlike many ossuaries, the bones in the Douaumont Ossuary aren't organized. They were purposely left in messy piles to remind visitors of the realities of war.

A Somber Reminder

After WWI, thousands upon thousands of bones were removed from the battlefield near Verdun and stored in a temporary ossuary. The Douaumont Ossuary was completed in 1927. Today, the ossuary and graveyard are a **somber** reminder of the evils of war. In 2008, people from many countries met there to remember the end of WWI. During a speech, French president Nicolas Sarkozy said that it was important to "honor all the dead, without exception."

GRAVE MATTERS

The Douaumont Ossuary is made up of 52 chambers. Each tomb holds bones collected from a particular area of the battlefield.

In 1975, the group Khmer Rouge took control of the country of Cambodia. They immediately forced citizens to become farmers in an effort to change the democratic country into a **communist** one. Between 1975 and 1979, the Khmer Rouge tortured and murdered nearly 2 million Cambodians. The areas where mass murders occurred are known as the Killing Fields. This was one of the worst **genocides** in human history.

The Khmer Rouge buried their victims in mass graves. In 1980, the remains of nearly 9,000 people were exhumed from graves in Choeung Ek. Many other graves were left alone. In 1988, the Memorial Stupa was built to hold more than 5,000 skulls retrieved from the graves. It's a quiet and peaceful place today, despite its horrific past.

Honoring the Innocent

The skulls of the Memorial Stupa are displayed in rows and piles inside glass cases. Many of the skulls are broken or have holes because Khmer Rouge soldiers often used farm tools to kill helpless men, women, and children. Of all the ossuaries mentioned in this book, the Memorial Stupa might be the most chilling. The display is meant to be a reminder of the horrors of war in the hope of avoiding future genocides.

Visitors can tour a museum at Choeung Ek containing the pictures of people who died there, as well as the stories of survivors. They can also see the pits where the remains were exhumed.
GRAVE MATTERS
A stupa is a Buddhist monument that holds ancient relics or the remains of important Buddhist figures.

AN OSSUARY MYSTERY

Some ossuaries are small boxes containing the remains of a single person. Around 2,000 years ago, ossuary boxes were a common way to save burial space. In the early 2000s, a small ossuary was found near Jerusalem, Israel. On the side, in an ancient language, are the words, "James, son of Joseph, brother of Jesus." Could this ossuary be proof that Jesus really lived 2,000 years ago?

The James Ossuary is proof of one thing for sure. People have been using ossuaries and charnel houses for centuries. The purposes may be different depending on the era, culture, or religion that produced them. However, they demonstrate a common human desire to remember and honor people of the past.

Real or Forgery?

Many people believe the James Ossuary is genuine proof that Jesus existed. Many others, however, believe while the box is 2,000 years old, some of the writing on the side was added many years later, making it a **forgery**. People who think it's real believe the writing was damaged while being studied. Whether it's real or a forgery, we may never know. What do you think?

The James Ossuary is made of chalk, a type of limestone. This was commonly used to make ossuary boxes around the time Jesus was said to have lived.

GRAVE MATTERS

The James Ossuary was empty when it was found, so there were no bones to study.

GLOSSARY

catacombs: underground passageways and rooms. Sometimes they contain tombs and bones.

communist: someone who practices communism, which is a government system in which the government controls what is used to make and transport products, and there is no privately owned property

decompose: to rot

exhume: to remove a body from where it is buried

forgery: a fake

friary: a monastery, or church, where monks called friars live

genocide: the purposeful and systematic killing of a cultural, religious, or political group of people

ghastly: horrible or shocking

inter: to put a dead body into a grave or tomb

medieval: having to do with the Middle Ages, a time in European history from about 500 to 1500

mortuary: related to death or the burial of the dead

profane: showing disrespect for religious things. Also, not religious.

quicklime: a white, solid chemical that can burn flesh

somber: sad and serious

vertebra: one of the 33 bones that make up the backbone. The plural form is "vertebrae."

FOR MORE INFORMATION

Books

Noyes, Deborah. *Encyclopedia of the End: Mysterious Death in Fact, Fancy, Folklore, and More.* Boston, MA: Houghton Mifflin, 2008.

Von Finn, Denny. *Paris Catacombs.* Minneapolis, MN: Bellwether Media, 2014.

Websites

Bones Don't Lie
bonesdontlie.wordpress.com
This is a fascinating blog written by an anthropology student who specializes in mortuary archaeology.

Empire de la Mort
empiredelamort.com
Visit this online resource for charnel houses and catacombs around the world to see amazing, up-close photographs of the bones they contain.

Publisher's note to educators and parents: Our editors have carefully reviewed these websites to ensure that they are suitable for students. Many websites change frequently, however, and we cannot guarantee that a site's future contents will continue to meet our high standards of quality and educational value. Be advised that students should be closely supervised whenever they access the Internet.

INDEX